THIS BOOK
BELONGS TO:

CUTE & PLAYFUL PATTERNS

Young
DREAMERS
PRESS

VISIT US ONLINE AT:
WWW.YOUNGDREAMERSPRESS.COM

CHECK US OUT ON FACEBOOK!
WWW.FACEBOOK.COM/YOUNGDREAMERSPRESS

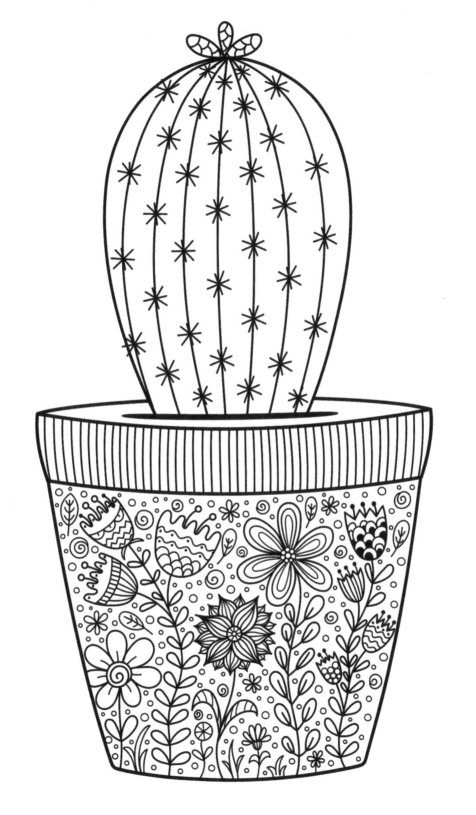

ALSO AVAILABLE

Unicorn Coloring Book: For Kids Ages 4-8
Softcover Paperback ISBN: 978-1989387962

CPSIA information can be obtained
at www.ICGtesting.com
Printed in the USA
LVHW052053160820
663297LV00001B/5